C000260113

ÖBB/AUSTRIAN FEDERAL RAILWAYS

SECOND EDITION

The complete guide to all ÖBB & Austrian
Independent Railways' Locomotives and Railcars

Brian Garvin & Peter Fox

Published by Platform 5 Publishing Ltd., Lydgate House, Lydgate Lane, Sheffield S10 5FH, England.

Printed by Bayliss Printing Co. Ltd., Turner Road, Worksop, Notts.

ISBN 0 906579 87-2

1110 001-3 at Innsbruck Hbf on 14/09/85 with the Westbound Venice–Simplon–Orient Express.

CONTENTS

Front Cover Photograph: 1044 501-3 arriving at Hohenau with a high-speed special from Wien Nord on 07/10/87. *Brian Garvin*

THE LOCOMOTIVE CLUB
OF GREAT BRITAIN

Thinking of going abroad? Austria? West Germany? Belgium? Holland? Luxembourg? France? Spain?

Well why not go with LCGB. Each year LCGB organises, for its members, tours to various European countries. Our steam specials are well known but did you know we also run modern traction tours?

In January 1989 we went to West Germany and visited many DB sheds as well as Bremen and Kassel workshops. At Easter we were in the Benelux countries. Other tours are planned for later in the year.

Each overseas tour includes train travel, shed and works visits and photographic opportunities. Why not join today. Also your Platform 5 overseas books can be kept up to date as our Club "Bulletin" features reports from most European countries.

Membership details can be obtained by sending an sae to J. Cramp, 8 Lovatt Close, Edgware, Middlesex, HA8 9XG.

INTRODUCTION

THE RAILWAYS OF AUSTRIA

Austria (Österreich in German) is a very mountainous country, and this is reflected in the fact that many of its main lines are curvy and hence severely speed-restricted, since they have to go up, down, around and through mountains. Because of this, journey times between centres can be long for the distances involved, but the scenic views are magnificent. There are some higher-speed routes, however, in the plain around Wien (Vienna).

As well as the Austrian State Railways (the Österreichische Bundesbahnen – ÖBB), there are also a number of independant railways owned either by the province, as in the case of the Steiermarkische Landesbahnen, the local authority as in the case of the SVB (Salzburg) or privately. There are also tramway systems (outside the scope of this book) in Wien (a tram-lovers paradise with over 1600 trams!), Graz, Innsbruck, Linz and Gmunden.

The state has had an involvement in the railways from quite early days, but there were many private companies whose initials crop up from time to time. Austria has had a chequered history which has had an effect on its railways. Over the years the state system has had various changes of title viz.

01/07/1884	kkStB	kaiserliche-königliche österreichische Staatsbahnen
12/11/1918	DÖStB	Deutschösterreichische Staatsbahnen
21/10/1919	ÖStB	Österreichische Staatsbahnen
01/04/1921	BBÖ	Bundesbahnen Österreich
18/03/1938	DRB	Deutsche Reichsbahn
27/04/1945	ÖStB	Österreichische Staatseisenbahn
05/08/1947	ÖBB	Österreichische Bundesbahnen

Some details of the old companies follow:

KEB. Kaiserin Elizabeth Bahn ('Westbahn').
KFJB. Kaiser Franz-Josefs Bahn
KFN. Kaiser Ferdinands Nordbahn.
KRB. Kronprinz Rudolf Bahn (St. Valentin/Amstetten–Selzthal–St. Michael–Villach–Tarvisio).
NÖLB. Niederösterreichische Landesbahnen (Korneuburg–Mistelbach–Hohenau, Stammersdorf–Dobermannsdorf and others).
NÖSWB. Niederösterreichische Südwestbahn (Leobersdorf–Hainfeld–St. Pölten, Pöchlarn–Kienberg Gaming and others).
ÖNWB. Österreichische Nordwestbahn (Wien–Retz–Praha).
SB. Südbahngesellschaft (Wien–Bruck a. d. Mur–Ljubljana–Trieste).
StEG. Österreichische-Ungarische Staatseisenbahngesellschaft ('Ostbahn').

DEVELOPMENTS

Three years have passed since the first edition of this book appeared. In that time ÖBB has continued to receive new electric locos, mostly of the cl. 1063, 1064 trip and shunting types which has allowed many older shunting locos to be withdrawn. EMU deliveries seem to have dried up for the time being but new DMUs are now being built which will mean the disappearance of the cl. 5081 railbuses and trailers, especially so since some lines were closed in 1988 allowing other types to be reallocated.

1987 saw Austria celebrating 150 years of railways and ÖBB really entered into the spirit of things by restoring to working order many historic locos and units and repainting selected locos from traffic stock into original liveries. The latter will probably continue to keep the old liveries and become museum locos in due course.

For the future ÖBB will receive some more 1044s, a few 1063s, 1064s and more 5047s. Some driving trailers are also be built for the 5047s. Plans are also being drawn up for new high speed lines and improvements to others for which new locos and EMUs will be built. Class designations 1047 and 4011 have been earmarked for these. A new dual voltage loco for the corridor service via San Candido will be designated cl. 1822 whilst a new diesel shunter is also contemplated which will become cl. 2068.

On the private lines the GySEV has showed the most change as electrification has been completed allowing many diesels to be sold to the MAV. Other lines are slowly obtaining new stock. In the case of SVB and WLB it is newly built, but Stern und Hafferl continue their tradition of obtaining second-hand stock.

ÖBB TRAIN SERVICES

These are classified as follows:

Ex (Expresszug) Express train (equivalent to German IC trains).
D (Schnellzug) Express train (generally to/from West Germany).
E (Eilzug) Semi-fast
EC Eurocity
R (Regionalzug) Stopping train

Supplements are payable for travel on D, Ex & EC trains.

Korridorzüge (corridor trains) are trains which pass through other countries without stopping for traffic purposes.

SOME COMMON RAILWAY TERMS

Lokomotive (Lok) – locomotive (loco).
Reisezugwagen – passenger coach.
Bahnsteig – platform.
Gleis – track.
Fahrkarte – ticket.
Hauptwerkstätte (abbreviated to HW) – works.
Direktion (abbreviated in Austria to Dion) – division.
Speisewagen – refreshment car.
Schlafwagen – sleeping car.
Liegewagen – couchette.
Dampflok – steam loco.
Ellok – electric loco.
Diesellok – diesel loco.
Schienenbus – railbus.
Bahnhof (abbreviated to Bhf) – station.
Hauptbahnhof (abbreviated to Hbf) – main station.
Hauptguterbahnhof (abbreviated to Hgbf) – main goods depot.
Verschiebebahnhof (abbreviated to Vbf) – marshalling yard.

LOCO & RAILCAR NUMBERING SYSTEM

The present ÖBB numbering scheme dates from 1953 when the former DRG system was replaced.

ÖBB locomotives and units had, until recently, a two-part number. The first part was of four digits and referred to the class of vehicle. It was separated by a full-stop from the second part which was the serial number within the particular type. Variations within a type were often given running numbers in a separate hundred. eg: 1042.01, 1042.501.

Early in 1985 the scheme was amended for use with computers. The running number part is now always 3 digits and there is an additional check digit suffix, e.g. 1020 026-9. The class number and serial number are separated by a space.

The class coding system refers to the type of vehicle & its use as follows:

1st digit Traction Code

0 Steam.
1 Electric Locomotives
2 Diesel Locomotives
3 Steam Railcars
4 Electric Multiple Units
5 Diesel Multiple Units
6 Driving Trailers (6000–6499 for EMUs, 6500–6999 for diesel railcars)
7 Intermediate Trailer
8 (Not used)
9 Tenders

2nd digit Origin Code

0–5 Austrian or German standard types. (0 was not carried on steam locomotives).
6–8 Pre-DRG types
9 Various Foreign types

This system was later amended for electric traction:

- 0–7 AC Electrics
- 8 AC/DC Electrics
- 9 DC Electrics

The second digit is also increased by 1 to represent developments of types. Thus class 1145 is a development of class 1045. 1245 is a further development of the same.

3rd & 4th digits Utilisation Code

Steam Locomotives	Electric Locomotives	Railcars
01–39 Passenger Tender	01–19 Express	01–19 Express
40–59 Freight Tender	20–39 Heavy Freight	20–59 Local
60–79 Passenger Tank	40–59 Mixed Traffic	60–79 Baggage
80–96 Freight Tank	60–69 Shunter	80–89 Light Railbus
97 Rack Fitted	70–89 Spare, but used	90–99 Narrow Gauge
98–99 Narrow Gauge	for old types	
	90–99 Narrow Gauge	

Diesel Locomotives

- 01–19 Express Passenger Locomotive over 2000hp
- 20–39 Heavy Freight Locomotive over 2000hp
- 40–59 Mixed Traffic Locomotive 1000-2000hp
- 60–64 "B" wheel arrangement locomotive under 1000hp
- 65–69 "C" wheel arrangement locomotive under 1000hp
- 70–79 "D" wheel arrangement locomotive under 1000hp
- 80–89 Free (was rack fitted locomotive) now used for self-propelled snowplough.
- 90–99 Narrow Gauge Locomotives

After the running number there is a computer check digit which double checks that all the preceding digits are correct. It is arrived at by multiplying the class and running number digits alternatively by 2 and 1. The resulting digits are added together and the sum deducted from the next whole ten gives the check number.

Example 1020 026-9

$$\begin{array}{ccccccc} 1 & 0 & 2 & 0 & 0 & 2 & 6 \\ \times\ 2 & 1 & 2 & 1 & 2 & 1 & 2 \end{array}$$

$$2+0+4+0+0+2+1+2 = 11$$

$$20 - 11 = 9$$

As these check numbers are actually carried on the locomotives and units they are included in this book.

So taking the example 1045 009-6. This is a mixed traffic electric locomotive. 1145 007-9 is an example of a class developed from class 1045, and 1245 004-5 is an example of a further development. 1245 509-3 is the first of a modified version of the latter, being fitted with rheostatic braking. Other examples are: 2062 061-3 is a four wheeled diesel shunter, 4010 010-9 is an express EMU.

VEHICLE TYPE CODES FOR RAILCARS & MULTIPLE UNITS

The abbreviations in common use in Austria are used, with the normal British codes in brackets. The Austrian codes are:

ET	Electric power car	A	1st Class
ES	Driving trailer for above	B	2nd Class
VT	Diesel power car	AB	Composite
VS	Driving trailer for above	D	Vehicle with luggage compartment
T	Trailer	4	Vehicle with 4 axles (instead of 2
h	Electric heating	BR	Buffet Car
I	Control wired	WR	Restaurant Car

Note—The continental system does not differentiate between open and compartment stock nor indicate toilet facilities.

British codes are also shown in brackets as follows:

D	Driving	F	First	O	Open
M	Motor	S	Second	K	Side Corridor
T	Trailer	C	Composite	RSS	Self-service Buffet
B	Brake	U	Unclassified	RUB	Restaurant Buffet
L	Lavatory	W	Washroom	RB	Buffet

The number of seats and lavatory compartments and are shown as nF nS nL e.g.: 80S 2L has 80 second class seats and two lavatory compartments.

DEPOTS

The ÖBB is divided into four divisions ('Direktionen'). In each division are several 'Zugförderungsleitungen' (Zf). These are depots with full maintenance facilities which are capable of carrying out heavy repairs. Other depots ('Zugförderungsstellen' – Zfs) only carry out lighter maintenance. These are shown on page 96 for convenience when using the book.

There are also several stabling points (often old steam depots). These are:

Innsbruck division: Innsbruck Hbf, Saalfelden, Wolfurt.
Linz division: Braunau, Hieflau, St. Valentin, Salzburg Hbf.
Villach division: Bruck a.d. Mür, Fehring, Klagenfurt, Spittal-Millstättersee, St. Veit a.d. Glan, Wolfsberg, Zeltweg.
Wien division: Bruck a. d. Leitha, Laa an der Thaya, Friedberg, Hohenau, Kledering Yard, Mistelbach, Schwarzenau, Sigmundsherberg.

WORKSHOPS

Workshops (Hauptwerkstätten) are as follows:

Floridsdorf: All EMUs and EMU trailers, some wagons.
Jedlersdorf: Wagons.
Knittelfeld: All steam locos, electric locos of cl.1061, 1062, 1067, diesel locos of classes 2043, 2060, 2062, 2067, 2080, 2180. Overhead line maintenance units (Motor tower wagons). Departmental rolling stock.
Linz: All electric locos except 1061, 1062, 1067, 1161.
St.Pölten: All diesel locos except cl.2043, 2060, 2062, 2067, 2080, 2180. All diesel raicars and trailers. All narrow gauge diesels. Standard and narrow gauge carriages. All tractors. Cranes. Departmental oberbauwagen.
Simmering: Carriages, luggage vans.
Wörth: Permanent way trolleys, points and crossings.

ACKNOWLEDGEMENTS

We would like to thank all who have helped in the production of this book, in particular Chris Appleby, Roland Beier, Peter Heppenstall and Karl Zochmeister.

The following references were consulted during its preparation:

Eisenbahnführer Österreich.
Eisenbahn.
Eisenbahn Kurier.
LCGB Bulletin.
LOK Report.
Schienenverkehr Aktuell.
ÖBB Handbook.
BBÖ Lokomotiv-Chronik 1923–1938. Slezak.

Information is updated to 01/01/89

ÖBB NETWORK MAP

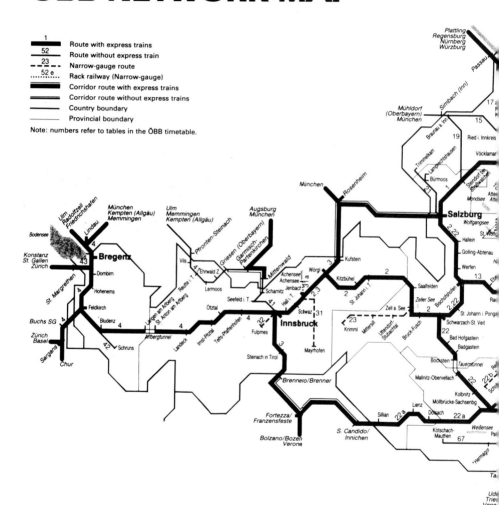

1	Route with express trains
52	Route without express train
23	Narrow-gauge route
52 e	Rack railway (Narrow-gauge)
▬▬▬	Corridor route with express trains
▬▬▬	Corridor route without express trains
───	Country boundary
───	Provincial boundary

Note: numbers refer to tables in the ÖBB timetable.

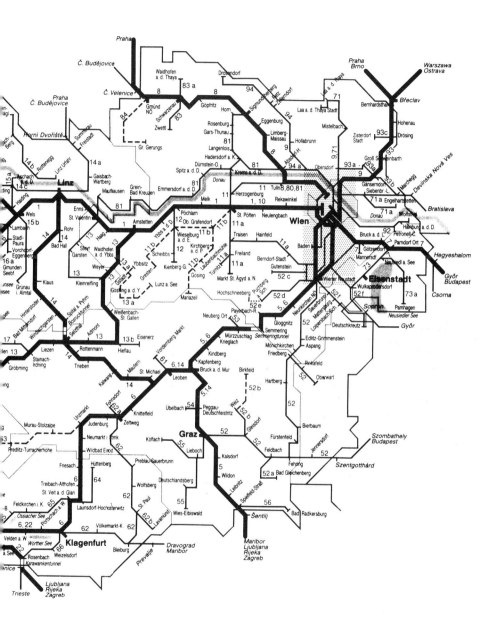

▲1010 012-1 awaits departure from Innsbruck with the 09.40 to Graz on 14/04/88.   *R.B.Arthur*
▼The 1018 class were developed from the DRG class E 18. Only five now survive. 1018 002-4 is seen at Wels on 09/11/86 with the 14.40 Wien Westbahnhof–Innsbruck. *Philip Wormald*

ELECTRIC LOCOMOTIVES

CLASS 1010   Co–Co

These locos are also based at Salzburg for mixed traffic duties over a wide area.

Built: 1955–58.
Builder-Mech Parts: Simmering-Graz-Pauker.
Builder-Elec. Parts: Brown-Boveri/Siemens/Elin.
One Hour Rating: 4000 kW.   **Weight in Full Working Order:** 106 tonnes.
Maximum Tractive Effort: 275 kN.   **Length over Buffers:** 17.86 m.
Driving Wheel Dia.: 1300 mm.   **Max. Speed:** 130 km/h.

1010 001-4	SB	1010 008-9	SB	1010 015-4	SB
1010 002-2	SB	1010 009-7	SB	1010 016-2	SB
1010 003-0	SB	1010 010-5	SB	1010 017-0	SB
1010 004-8	SB	1010 011-3	SB	1010 018-8	SB
1010 005-5	SB	1010 012-1	SB	1010 019-6	SB
1010 006-3	SB	1010 013-9	SB	1010 020-4	SB
1010 007-1	SB	1010 014-7	SB		

CLASS 1110   Bo–Bo

Based in Innsbrück and Bludenz, this class can be found on all routes in the Tirol, Brenner and Vorarlberg areas, and as far east as Salzburg. Each depot has some through workings to Wien on overnight freights, one Innsbruck loco normally returning on a daytime freight. The 1110.5s are normally confined to the mountain lines.

Built: 1956–60.
Builder-Mech Parts: Simmering-Graz-Pauker.
Builder-Elec. Parts: Brown Boveri/Elin/Siemens.
Weight in Full Working Order: 106 tonnes (1110.0). 114 tonnes(1110.5).
Maximum Tractive Effort: 275 kN.   **One Hour Rating:** 4000 kW.
Driving Wheel Dia.: 1300 mm.   **Length over Buffers:** 17.86 m.
Max. Speed: 110 km/h.   **Electric Braking:** Rheostatic (1110.5 only).

1110 001-3	IN	1110 014-6	IN	1110 505-3	BL
1110 003-9	IN	1110 015-3	IN	1110 516-0	BL
1110 004-7	IN	1110 017-9	IN	1110 519-4	BL
1110 006-2	IN	1110 018-7	IN	1110 521-0	BL
1110 007-0	IN	1110 020-3	IN	1110 522-8	BL
1110 008-8	IN	1110 023-7	IN	1110 524-4	BL
1110 009-6	IN	1110 025-2	IN	1110 526-9	BL
1110 010-4	IN	1110 027-8	IN	1110 529-3	BL
1110 011-2	IN	1110 028-6	IN	1110 530-1	BL
1110 012-0	IN	1110 502-0	BL		

CLASS 1018   1–Do–1

The 1018s were built in Austria during the war as DRG E 18 201–8. They were returned to Austria after the war, and have about three more years to run before withdrawal. They have been modified with new cab windscreens and headlights and can still be found on express duties as well as local passenger on the routes from Linz to Salzburg/Passau and Kleinreifling.

Built: 1939.
Builder-Mech Parts: Floridsdorf.
Builder-Elec. Parts: AEG /Siemens.
One Hour Rating: 3340 kW.   **Weight in Full Working Order:** 110 tonnes.
Maximum Tractive Effort: 196 kN.   **Length over Buffers:** 16.92 m.
Driving Wheel Dia.: 1600 mm.   **Max. Speed:** 130 km/h.

1018 002-4	LZ	1018 007-3	LZ	1018 008-1	LZ
1018 004-0	LZ				

Two class 1020s (originally DRG class E 94) Nos. 1020 037-6 and 1020 029-3 provide super power on 27/02/89 for the 15.44 St. Anton–Bludenz.
Graham Scott-Lowe

CLASS 1020   Co–Co

This class was inherited from the Deutsche Reichsbahn at the end of the second world war (Class E 94). Other examples are still at work in East Germany (Class 254), but the ÖBB locos have been rebuilt with modified cabs and headlights. A further three examples were built in Austria at Floridsdorf in 1954 (1020.45–47), and it is perhaps significant that these were the first to be withdrawn! The Innsbrück and Wörgl locos are found on wide ranging duties between Lindau and Salzburg, Innsbrück and Brennero and Innsbruck to Kufstein. Those at Bludenz have some local passenger duties to Bregenz and St.Anton am Arlberg but also see use as pilot locos on the arduous stretch of the Arlberg route route between Bludenz and Landeck. The Villach locos will be found working to Jesenice, Arnoldstein and Tarvisio.

Built: 1940–44.
Builder-Mech Parts: Krauss-Maffei /AEG.
Builder-Elec. Parts: Siemens /AEG.
One Hour Rating: 3300 kW.   **Weight in Full Working Order:** 118.5 tonnes.
Maximum Tractive Effort: 314 kN.   **Length over Buffers:** 18.60 m.
Driving Wheel Dia.: 1250 mm.   **Max. Speed:** 90 km/h.

Former DRG numbers in parentheses.

1020 001-2 (E94.008)	IN	1020 024-4 (E94.025)	VH
1020 003-8 (E94.011)	IN	1020 025-1 (E94.027)	VH
1020 004-6 (E94.029)	IN	1020 026-9 (E94.028)	VH
1020 005-3 (E94.030)	IN	1020 027-7 (E94.061)	VH
1020 006-1 (E94.031)	IN	1020 028-5 (E94.064)	BL
1020 007-9 (E94.033)	IN	1020 029-3 (E94.068)	BL
1020 008-7 (E94.034)	IN	1020 030-1 (E94.075)	BL
1020 009-5 (E94.037)	IN	1020 031-9 (E94.076)	BL
1020 010-3 (E94.088)	IN	1020 032-7 (E94.078)	BL
1020 011-1 (E94.090)	WL	1020 033-5 (E94.094)	BL
1020 012-9 (E94.123)	WL	1020 034-3 (E94.095)	BL
1020 013-7 (E94.127)	WL	1020 035-0 (E94.097)	BL
1020 014-5 (E94.129)	WL	1020 037-6 (E94.099)	BL
1020 015-2 (E94.130)	WL	1020 038-4 (E94.100)	BL
1020 016-0 (E94.134)	WL	1020 039-2 (E94.101)	BL
1020 017-8 (E94.135)	VH	1020 040-0 (E94.102)	BL
1020 018-6 (E94.001)	VH	1020 041-8 (E94.103)	BL
1020 020-2 (E94.003)	VH	1020 042-6 (E94.104)	BL
1020 022-8 (E94.005)	VH	1020 044-2 (E94.136)	BL
1020 023-6 (E94.006)	VH		

CLASS 1040   Bo–Bo

The main use for these locos is now light freight and shunting duties often well away from their own area. AM locos will be found at Krems, Waidhofen a.d. Ybbs, Amstetten and St.Pölten. MZ locos are found at Wiener Neustadt, Stadlau, Krems, Tulln, and Mürzzuschlag.

Built: 1950–52.
Builder-Mech Parts: Floridsdorf.
Builder-Elec. Parts: Elin.
One Hour Rating: 2340 kW.   **Weight in Full Working Order:** 80 tonnes.
Maximum Tractive Effort: 196 kN.   **Length over Buffers:** 12.92 m.
Driving Wheel Dia.: 1350 mm.   **Max. Speed:** 90 km/h.

1040 001-8	MZ	1040 007-5	MZ	1040 012-5	AM
1040 002-6	AM	1040 008-3	MZ	1040 013-3	AM
1040 003-4	MZ	1040 009-1	MZ	1040 014-1	AM
1040 004-2	MZ	1040 010-9	MZ	1040 015-8	AM
1040 005-9	MZ	1040 011-7	AM	1040 016-6	AM
1040 006-7	MZ				

CLASS 1041 Bo–Bo

These locos. work local freight and passenger trains between Linz, Attnang Puchheim and Stainach Irdning and Bischofshofen–Selzthal/Salzburg.

Built: 1952–54.
Builder-Mech Parts: Simmering-Graz-Pauker.
Builder-Elec. Parts: Siemens/Brown-Boveri/AEG.
One Hour Rating: 2360 kW.   **Weight in Full Working Order:** 83.8 tonnes.
Maximum Tractive Effort: 196 kN.   **Length over Buffers:** 15.32 m.
Driving Wheel Dia.: 1350 mm.   **Max. Speed:** 80 km/h.

1041 001-7	BO	1041 009-0	AT	1041 018-1	AT
1041 002-5	AT	1041 010-8	AT	1041 019-9	AT
1041 003-3	AT	1041 011-6	AT	1041 020-7	AT
1041 004-1	AT	1041 012-4	AT	1041 022-3	AT
1041 005-8	BO	1041 013-2	AT	1041 023-1	AT
1041 006-6	BO	1041 015-7	AT	1041 024-9	AT
1041 007-4	BO	1041 016-5	AT	1041 025-6	AT
1041 008-2	AT	1041 017-3	AT		

CLASS 1141 Bo–Bo

Development of class 1041 used on local passenger trains Linz–Stainach Irdning/ Selzthal/Passau, Linz–Salzburg/Tauern line/Zell am See.

Built: 1955–57.
Builder-Mech Parts: Simmering-Graz-Pauker.
Builder-Elec. Parts: Siemens/AEG/Elin.
One Hour Rating: 2480 kW.   **Weight in Full Working Order:** 83 tonnes.
Maximum Tractive Effort: 196 kN.   **Length over Buffers:** 15.26 m.
Driving Wheel Dia.: 1300 mm.   **Max. Speed:** 110 km/h.

1141 001-6	AT	1141 011-5	LZ	1141 021-4	AT
1141 002-4	AT	1141 012-3	LZ	1141 022-2	AT
1141 003-2	AT	1141 013-1	LZ	1141 023-0	AT
1141 004-0	AT	1141 014-9	LZ	1141 024-8	AT
1141 005-7	AT	1141 015-6	LZ	1141 025-5	AT
1141 006-5	AT	1141 016-4	LZ	1141 026-3	AT
1141 007-3	AT	1141 017-2	LZ	1141 027-1	AT
1141 008-1	AT	1141 018-0	AT	1141 028-9	AT
1141 009-9	AT	1141 019-8	AT	1141 029-7	AT
1141 010-7	AT	1141 020-6	AT	1141 030-5	AT

CLASS 1042 Bo–Bo

Mixed traffic locos. with duties over all lines. There are some 1042.0 at Villach fitted with automatic couplings for working car trains from Mallnitz to Bockstein. 1042 652 was scrapped after an accident at Lambach on 18/09/87. 1042 044 was restored to original green livery for the ÖBB 150 celebrations.

Built: 1963–77.
Builder-Mech Parts: Simmering-Graz-Pauker.
Builder-Elec. Parts: Elin/Siemens/Brown-Boveri.
One Hour Rating: 3560 or 4000 kW.   **Weight in Full Working Order:** 83.8 tonnes.
Maximum Tractive Effort: 255 kN.   **Length over Buffers:** 16.22 m.
Driving Wheel Dia.: 1250 mm.   **Max. Speed:** 130 or 150 km/h.
Electric Brake: Rheostatic (Class 1042.5 only).

Class 1042.0. 3560 kW. 130 km/h.

1042 001-6	WW	1042 008-1	WW	1042 015-6	WW
1042 002-4	WW	1042 009-9	WW	1042 016-4	KD
1042 003-2	WW	1042 010-7	WW	1042 017-2	KD
1042 004-0	WW	1042 011-5	WW	1042 018-0	KD
1042 005-7	WW	1042 012-3	WW	1042 019-8	KD
1042 006-5	WW	1042 013-1	WW	1042 020-6	KD
1042 007-3	WW	1042 014-9	WW	1042 021-4	KD

1042 022-2	KD	1042 035-4	LZ	1042 048-7	LZ
1042 023-0	KD	1042 036-2	LZ	1042 049-5	LZ
1042 024-8	KD	1042 037-0	LZ	1042 050-3	LZ
1042 025-5	KD	1042 038-8	LZ	1042 051-1	LZ
1042 026-3	KD	1042 039-6	LZ	1042 052-9	LZ
1042 027-1	KD	1042 040-4	LZ	1042 053-7	LZ
1042 028-9	AM	1042 041-2	LZ	1042 054-5	LZ
1042 029-7	AM	1042 042-0	LZ	1042 055-2	LZ
1042 030-5	AM	1042 043-8	LZ	1042 056-0	LZ
1042 031-3	AM	1042 044-6 G	LZ	1042 057-8 G	LZ
1042 032-1	AM	1042 045-3	LZ	1042 058-6	LZ
1042 033-9	AM	1042 046-1	LZ	1042 059-4	LZ
1042 034-7	LZ	1042 047-9	LZ	1042 060-2	LZ

Class 1042.5. 4000 kW. 150 km/h. Fitted with rheostatic braking.

1042 501-5	GZ	1042 562-7	LZ	1042 612-0	BO
1042 502-3	GZ	1042 563-5	LZ	1042 613-8	BO
1042 503-1	GZ	1042 564-3	LZ	1042 614-6	VH
1042 504-9	GZ	1042 565-0	LZ	1042 615-3	VH
1042 505-6	GZ	1042 566-8	LZ	1042 616-1	VH
1042 506-4	GZ	1042 567-6	LZ	1042 617-9	VH
1042 508-0	GZ	1042 568-4	LZ	1042 618-7	VH
1042 509-8 G	GZ	1042 569-2	LZ	1042 619-5	VH
1042 510-6	GZ	1042 570-0	LZ	1042 620-3	VH
1042 511-4	GZ	1042 571-8	LZ	1042 621-1	VH
1042 512-2	GZ	1042 572-6	LZ	1042 622-9	VH
1042 513-0	GZ	1042 573-4	LZ	1042 623-7	VH
1042 514-8	GZ	1042 574-2	LZ	1042 624-5	VH
1042 515-5	GZ	1042 575-9	LZ	1042 625-2	VH
1042 516-3	GZ	1042 576-7	MZ	1042 626-0	VH
1042 517-1	GZ	1042 577-5	MZ	1042 627-8	VH
1042 518-9	GZ	1042 578-3	MZ	1042 628-6	VH
1042 519-7	GZ	1042 579-1	MZ	1042 629-4	VH
1042 520-5	GZ	1042 580-9	MZ	1042 630-2	VH
1042 531-2	GZ	1042 581-7	MZ	1042 631-0	VH
1042 532-0	GZ	1042 582-5	MZ	1042 632-8	VH
1042 533-8	GZ	1042 583-3	MZ	1042 633-6	VH
1042 534-6	GZ	1042 584-1	MZ	1042 634-4	VH
1042 535-3	GZ	1042 585-8	MZ	1042 635-1	VH
1042 536-1	GZ	1042 586-6	MZ	1042 636-9	VH
1042 537-9	GZ	1042 587-4	MZ	1042 637-7	SB
1042 538-7	GZ	1042 588-2	MZ	1042 638-5	SB
1042 539-5	GZ	1042 589-0	MZ	1042 639-3	SB
1042 540-3	GZ	1042 590-8	MZ	1042 640-1	SB
1042 541-1	GZ	1042 591-6	MZ	1042 641-9	SB
1042 542-9	GZ	1042 592-4	MZ	1042 642-7	SB
1042 543-7	GZ	1042 593-2	MZ	1042 643-5	SB
1042 544-5	GZ	1042 594-0	MZ	1042 644-3	WW
1042 545-2	GZ	1042 595-7	MZ	1042 645-0	WW
1042 546-0	GZ	1042 596-5	MZ	1042 646-8	WW
1042 547-8	GZ	1042 597-3	MZ	1042 647-6	WW
1042 548-6	GZ	1042 598-1	MZ	1042 648-4	WW
1042 549-4	GZ	1042 599-9	MZ	1042 649-2	WW
1042 550-2	GZ	1042 600-5	BO	1042 650-0	WW
1042 551-0	GZ	1042 601-3	BO	1042 651-8	WW
1042 552-8	GZ	1042 602-1	BO	1042 653-4	WW
1042 553-6	GZ	1042 603-9	BO	1042 654-2	WW
1042 554-4	GZ	1042 604-7	BO	1042 655-9	WW
1042 555-1	GZ	1042 605-4	BO	1042 656-7	WW
1042 556-9	WW	1042 606-2	BO	1042 657-5	WW
1042 557-7	WW	1042 607-0	BO	1042 658-3	WW
1042 558-5	WW	1042 608-8	BO	1042 659-1	WW
1042 559-3	WW	1042 609-6	BO	1042 660-9	WW
1042 560-1	WW	1042 610-4	BO	1042 661-7	WW
1042 561-9	LZ	1042 611-2	BO	1042 662-5	WW

◄Although built in 1950, the class 1040 has bogies of a similar style to the pre-war class 1245. 1040 001-8 is seen at Wiener Neustadt on 16/09/87.
Colin Boocock

▼Triple-headers are unusual in most countries, but they do occur in Austria, although it is unusual for all three to be of the same class! 1044 105-3, 1044 064-2 and 1044 060-0 are seen passing Breitenstein on the Semmering line with the 'Gondolieri' from Venezia to Wien Südbahnhof on 15/09/87.
Colin Boocock

1042 663-3	WW	1042 678-1	WS	1042 693-0	WS
1042 664-1	WW	1042 679-9	WS	1042 694-8	WS
1042 665-8	WS	1042 680-7	WS	1042 695-5	WS
1042 666-6	WS	1042 681-5	WS	1042 696-3	WS
1042 667-4	WS	1042 682-3	WS	1042 697-1	WS
1042 668-2	WS	1042 683-1	WS	1042 698-9	WS
1042 669-0	WS	1042 684-9	WS	1042 699-7	WS
1042 670-8	WS	1042 685-6	WS	1042 700-3	WS
1042 671-6	WS	1042 686-4	WS	1042 701-1	WS
1042 672-4	WS	1042 687-2	WS	1042 702-9	WS
1042 673-2	WS	1042 688-0	WS	1042 703-7	WS
1042 674-0	WS	1042 689-8	WS	1042 704-5	WS
1042 675-7	WS	1042 690-6	WS	1042 705-2	WS
1042 676-5	WS	1042 691-4	WS	1042 706-0	WS
1042 677-3	WS	1042 692-2	WS	1042 ˙07-8	WS

CLASS 1043 Bo–Bo

These locos are the Swedish Railways class Rc2 and until recently all carried the SJ style livery. They were ordered as prototypes to assess the benefits of thyristor control and after extensive trials provided much useful experience for the production series of class 1044. During the last two years most locos have been through the shops and received refurbishment and changed liveries. The class is found in mixed traffic over the Tauern line.

Built: 1971–73.
Builder-Mech Parts: Nohab, Falun, Hägglund.
Builder-Elec. Parts: ASEA.
One Hour Rating: 3600 (4000*) kW. **Weight in Full Working Order**: 83.2 (77.4*) tonnes.
Maximum Tractive Effort: 294 kN. **Length over Buffers**: 15.58 m.
Driving Wheel Dia.: 1300 mm **Max. Speed**: 135 km/h.
Electric Brake:Rheostatic.*§

1043 001-5 J *	VH	1043 005-6 N	VH	1043 008-0	VH
1043 002-3 *	VH	1043 006-4 N	VH	1043 009-8	VH
1043 003-1 J *	VH	1043 007-2	VH	1043 010-6 N	VH
1043 004-9 J §	VH				

CLASS 1044 Bo–Bo

The Austrian development of the Swedish-built class 1043. The class has grown rapidly over the last 11 years and can be found on mixed traffic duties on all main lines and some branches. The express passenger duties take them into West Germany where they work through to Frankfurt am Main via Passau and München via Rosenheim. Fifteen more locos have recently been ordered of a new sub series. 1044 201–215 are due for delivery 4/89–4/90. In 1987 1044 001 was rebuilt for high speed running and renumbered to 1044 501.

Built: 1974 onwards.
Builder-Mech Parts: Simmering-Graz-Pauker.
Builder-Elec. Parts: Brown-Boveri/Elin/Siemens.
One Hour Rating: 5300 kW. **Weight in Full Working Order**: 83 tonnes.
Maximum Tractive Effort: 314 kN. **Length over Buffers**: 16.00 m.
Driving Wheel Dia.: 1300 mm. **Max. Speed**: 160 km/h (*220 km/h).
Non-Standard Livery: 1044 501 is as shown on the front cover of this book.

1044 002-2	WS	1044 014-7	SB	1044 026-1	SB
1044 003-0	SB	1044 015-4	SB	1044 027-9	SB
1044 004-8	SB	1044 016-2	SB	1044 028-7	SB
1044 005-5	SB	1044 017-0	SB	1044 029-5	SB
1044 006-3	SB	1044 018-8	SB	1044 030-3	SB
1044 007-1	SB	1044 019-6	SB	1044 031-1	SB
1044 008-9	SB	1044 020-4	SB	1044 032-9	SB
1044 009-7	SB	1044 021-2	SB	1044 033-7	VH
1044 010-5	SB	1044 022-0	SB	1044 034-5	VH
1044 011-3	SB	1044 023-8	SB	1044 035-2	VH
1044 012-1	SB	1044 024-6	SB	1044 036-0	VH
1044 013-9	SB	1044 025-3	SB	1044 037-8	VH

◄Only three members of class 1145 survive. 1145 008-7 is seen at Landeck shed on 27/02/89.
Graham Scott-Lowe

▼Electric shunter 1062 003-7 shunts the stock of the eastbound Orient Express at Wien Westbahnhof on 27/07/87.
R.B. Arthur

1044 039-4	VH	1044 074-1	BL	1044 109-5	WW
1044 040-2	VH	1044 075-8	BL	1044 110-3	WW
1044 041-0	VH	1044 076-6	BL	1044 111-1	WW
1044 042-8	VH	1044 077-4	BL	1044 112-9	WW
1044 043-6	VH	1044 078-2	BL	1044 113-7	WW
1044 044-4	VH	1044 079-0	BL	1044 114-5	WW
1044 045-1	VH	1044 080-8	BL	1044 115-2	WW
1044 046-9	VH	1044 081-6	BL	1044 116-0	WW
1044 047-7	LZ	1044 082-4	BL	1044 117-8 N	WW
1044 048-5	LZ	1044 083-2	BL	1044 118-6	WW
1044 049-3	LZ	1044 084-0	IN	1044 119-4	WW
1044 050-1	LZ	1044 085-7	IN	1044 120-2	WW
1044 051-9	LZ	1044 086-5	IN	1044 121-0	WW
1044 052-7	LZ	1044 087-3	IN	1044 122-8	WW
1044 053-5	LZ	1044 088-1	IN	1044 123-6	WW
1044 054-3	LZ	1044 089-9	IN	1044 124-4	WW
1044 055-0	LZ	1044 090-7	IN	1044 125-1	WW
1044 056-8	LZ	1044 091-5	IN	1044 126-9	WW
1044 057-6	WS	1044 092-3 N	IN	1044 201-0	
1044 058-4	WS	1044 093-1	IN	1044 202-8	
1044 059-2	WS	1044 094-9	IN	1044 203-6	
1044 060-0	WS	1044 095-6	IN	1044 204-4	
1044 061-8	WS	1044 096-4	IN	1044 205-1	
1044 062-6	WS	1044 097-2	IN	1044 206-9	
1044 063-4	WS	1044 098-0	IN	1044 207-7	
1044 064-2	WS	1044 099-8	IN	1044 208-5	
1044 065-9	WS	1044 100-4	IN	1044 209-3	
1044 066-7	WS	1044 101-2	IN	1044 210-1	
1044 067-5	WS	1044 102-0	WS	1044 211-9	
1044 068-3	WS	1044 103-8	WS	1044 212-7	
1044 069-1	WS	1044 104-6	WS	1044 213-5	
1044 070-9	VH	1044 105-3	WS	1044 214-3	
1044 071-7	BL	1044 106-1	WS	1044 215-0	
1044 072-5	BL	1044 107-9	WW	1044 501-6 N *	WS
1044 073-3	BL	1044 108-7	WW		

CLASS 1045   Bo–Bo

The survivors of this venerable class are to be found on local freight duties and shunting at Neumarkt Kallham and Vöcklabrück. 1045.01 and 03 are now operated by the Montafonerbahn. 1045 009 was restored to green livery in 1987 as part of ÖBB 150 Celebrations.

Built: 1927–28.
Builder-Mech Parts: Wiener Neustadt/Floridsdorf.
Builder-Elec. Parts: Elin.
One Hour Rating: 1140 kW.
Maximum Tractive Effort: 150 kN.
Driving Wheel Dia.: 1300 mm.
Weight in Full Working Order: 61.2 tonnes.
Length over Buffers: 10.40 m.
Max. Speed: 60 km/h.

1045 009-6 G	AT	1045 012-0 G	AT	1045 014-6	AT

CLASS 1145   Bo–Bo

Development of class 1045. Also used on local freight and pilot duties at Wörgl and Innsbruck.

Built: 1927–31.
Builder-Mech Parts: Floridsdorf/Krauss.
Builder-Elec. Parts: Elin.
One Hour Rating: 1200 kW.
Maximum Tractive Effort: 175 kN.
Driving Wheel Dia.: 1300 mm.
Electric Braking: Regenerative.
Weight in Full Working Order: 70.6 (67) tonnes.
Length over Buffers: 11.88 m.
Max. Speed: 70 km/h.

1145 002-0 G *	IN	1145 011-1 G	IN	1145 014-5 G	IN
1145 008-7	IN				

CLASS 1245   Bo–Bo

KD locos are mostly used on local freight and pilot duties in a wide area of Steiermark including such places as Selzthal, Graz, Leoben, Vordernberg, Kapfenberg, Unzmarkt, Zeltweg and St. Michael. They also appear on certain local passenger trains from Leoben to Vordernberg and perhaps Leoben/Knittelfeld–Selzthal. The SL locos see use on local freights and pilot duties around Hieflau, Eisenerz and St. Valentin. WL locos are often used for assisting trains to Saalfelden where they also shunt. Another class whose duties are being affected by deliveries of new cl.1063s.

Built: 1934 (1245.0) 1938–40 (1245.5).
Builder-Mech Parts: Floridsdorf.
Builder-Elec. Parts: Brown-Boveri/Elin/Siemens-Wien/AEG.
One Hour Rating: 1840 kW.   **Weight in Full Working Order:** 83 tonnes.
Maximum Tractive Effort: 196 kN.   **Length over Buffers:** 12.92 m.
Driving Wheel Dia.: 1350 mm.   **Max. Speed:** 80 km/h.

1245 001-1	WL	1245 514-3 **G**	VH	1245 530-9	KD
1245 002-9	SL	1245 516-8	VH	1245 531-7	KD
1245 003-7	WL	1245 518-4	VH	1245 532-5	WL
1245 004-5	WL	1245 519-2	VH	1245 533-3	KD
1245 005-2 **G**	SL	1245 520-8 **G**	VH	1245 534-1	SL
1245 007-8	SL	1245 522-6	KD	1245 535-8	WL
1245 008-6	SL	1245 523-4 **G**	KD	1245 536-6	KD
1245 509-3	SL	1245 524-2	KD	1245 537-4	KD
1245 511-9	VH	1245 525-9	KD	1245 540-8	KD
1245 512-7	VH	1245 527-5	KD	1245 541-6	KD
1245 513-5	VH	1245 529-1	KD		

CLASS 1046   Bo–Bo

Although classed as locomotives these vehicles are in fact driving motor luggage vans and were previously classed as electric railcars and numbered in the 4061 series. Now the class is undergoing mid life refurbishment. Two locomotives have been rebuilt to class 1146, whilst 1046 025 had been used for some years as a test bed for three-phase motors, and was later renumbered 1046 023 when that loco was scrapped. Now it has been completely rebuilt and no longer has a luggage compartment. A standard cab has also been fitted. More locos are being rebuilt at the rate of two per year. Most of the WN locos surprisingly retain their green livery and work between Wien and Krems/Bruck a.d. Leitha/Mistelbach/ Bernhardsthal/Wiener Neustadt. AM locos also work from Wien to Krems but also reach Wien via the direct main line. They also work to Selzthal and Linz and branches in between. A plan to rebuild some into dual voltage locos for the Lienz–San Candido–Innsbruck route has been abandoned. 1046 005 was restored to original condition for the 1987 Celebrations.

Built: 1956–59.
Builder-Mech Parts: SGP/Floridsdorf.
Builder-Elec. Parts: Elin/AEG/Siemens.
One Hour Rating: 1600 kW.   **Weight in Full Working Order:** 67 tonnes.
Maximum Tractive Effort: 118 kN.   **Length over Buffers:** 16.17 m.
Driving Wheel Dia.: 1040 mm.   **Max. Speed:** 125 (140 r) km/h.

r Rebuilt with new body.

1046 001-2 **G**	WN	1046 009-5 **N** r	WN	1046 019-4 **G**	AM
1046 002-0	WN	1046 012-9 **G**	WN	1046 020-2	AM
1046 004-6 **G**	WN	1046 013-7 **G**	WN	1046 021-0	AM
1046 005-3 **G**	WN	1046 015-2	AM	1046 022-8	AM
1046 006-1 **G**	WN	1046 016-0	AM	1046 023-6 **N** r	AM
1046 007-9 **N** r	WN	1046 018-6	AM	1046 024-4	AM
1046 008-7 **G**	WN				

CLASS 1146   Bo–Bo

In 1987 two 1046s were completely rebuilt into dual voltage locomotives. The luggage compartment was done away with and a modern cab provided. These two locomotives are fitted out for working on 15 kV and 25 kV, the latter for working into Hungary. One loco is now regularly diagrammed to work the EC 'Lehar' throughout from Wien to Budapest. The train has been accelerated and is the first EC train in the Eastern Bloc.

Built: 1987.
Builder-Mech Parts: ÖBB HW Linz.
Builder-Elec. Parts: Elin.

One Hour Rating: 2000 kW.	**Weight in Full Working Order:** 76 tonnes.
Maximum Tractive Effort: 120 kN.	**Length over Buffers:** 16.23 m.
Driving Wheel Dia.: 1040 mm.	**Max. Speed:** 125 km/h.
Electric Brake: Regenerative.	**Systems:** 15 kV 16⅔ Hz/25 kV 50 Hz.

1146 001-1 (1046 003-8) **N**   WS |1146 002-9 (1046 017-8) **N**   WS

CLASS 1061   D

These shunters are used at Innsbruck Hbf, Innsbruck West (IN locos) and at Wörgl, Saalfelden and Kufstein (WL locos). 1061 002 was restored to original livery for the 1987 Celebrations.

Built: 1926.
Builder-Mech Parts: Floridsdorf.
Builder-Elec. Parts: AEG.

One Hour Rating: 720 kW.	**Weight in Full Working Order:** 54.8 tonnes.
Maximum Tractive Effort: 134 kN.	**Length over Buffers:** 10.00 m.
Driving Wheel Dia.: 1140 mm.	**Max. Speed:** 40 km/h.

1061 001-2	IN	1061 003-8	WL	1061 004-6	WL
1061 002-0 **G**	WL				

CLASS 1161   D

A shunting loco. Those at Innsbruck share duties with class 1061. Villach locos will be found at Villach Hbf, Villach West, Spittal and St. Veit a.d. Glan. The Bischofshofen locos are normally at Bischofshofen and Schwarzach St.Veit. Duties are now changing as cl. 1063s are introduced. The new marshalling yard at Fürnitz (Villach) will also mean workings will be rationalised in that area.

Built: 1928–40.
Builder-Mech Parts: Floridsdorf.
Builder-Elec. Parts: AEG/Siemens .

One Hour Rating: 700 kW.	**Weight in Full Working Order:** 56 tonnes.
Maximum Tractive Effort: 137 kN.	**Length over Buffers:** 10.50 m.
Driving Wheel Dia.: 1140 mm.	**Max. Speed:** 40 km/h.

1161 002-9 **G**	IN	1161 014-4 **G**	IN	1161 019-3	BO
1161 004-5	IN	1161 015-1	VH	1161 020-1	BO
1161 006-0	IN	1161 016-9 **G**	IN	1161 021-9	BO
1161 011-0 **G**	VH	1161 017-7	BO	1161 022-7	SB
1161 013-6	VH	1161 018-5	BO		

CLASS 1062   C

A shunting loco found in many yards around Wien such as Wien Süd, Wien Zentralvbf, Penzing, Hütteldorf and Schwechat. 1062 007 was restored to original livery for the 1987 celebrations.

Built: 1955.
Builder-Mech Parts: Floridsdorf.
Builder-Elec. Parts: AEG/Siemens.

One Hour Rating: 660 kW.	**Weight in Full Working Order:** 68 tonnes.
Maximum Tractive Effort: 186 kN.	**Length over Buffers:** 10.82 m.
Driving Wheel Dia.: 1140 mm.	**Max. Speed:** 50 km/h.

1062 001-1	WS	1062 005-2	WS	1062 009-4	WS
1062 002-9	WS	1062 006-0	WS	1062 010-2	WS
1062 003-7	WS	1062 007-8 **G**	WS	1062 011-0	WS
1062 004-5	WS	1062 008-6	WS	1062 012-8	WS

CLASS 1063   Bo–Bo

A dual-voltage shunting and trip loco featuring three-phase motors. These locos are now appearing in a number of main centres and may mean the withdrawal of older shunting locos. They see use on 25 kV electrification in Czechoslovakia and Hungary although there are no booked workings as yet to the latter country. Two to three WS locos are outbased at Hohenau for tripping freights into Czechoslovakia and they also work the cross border passenger trains! The other WS locos shunt at Wien Kledering yard. Locos from the other depots are normally found in the various freight yards around the towns concerned. 1063 038–049 are for delivery 9/89–2/91.

Built: 1982 onwards.
Builder-Mech Parts: Simmering-Graz-Pauker.
Builder-Elec. Parts: Brown Boveri/Siemens/Elin.
Continuous Rating: 2000 kW.   **Weight in Full Working Order:** 75.5 tonnes.
Maximum Tractive Effort: 260 kN   **Length over Buffers:** 15.56 m.
Driving Wheel Dia.: 1145 mm.   **Max. Speed:** 100 km/h.
Systems: 15 kV 16⅔ Hz/25 kV 50 Hz.

1063 001-0	WS	1063 018-4	SB	1063 034-1	IN
1063 002-8	IN	1063 019-2	SB	1063 035-8	WS
1063 003-6	WS	1063 020-0	SB	1063 036-6	WS
1063 004-4	WS	1063 021-8	SB	1063 037-4	WS
1063 005-1	WS	1063 022-6	SB	1063 038-2	
1063 006-9	VH	1063 023-4	SB	1063 039-0	
1063 007-7	VH	1063 024-2	LZ	1063 040-8	
1063 008-5	GZ	1063 025-9	LZ	1063 041-6	
1063 009-3	GZ	1063 026-7	LZ	1063 042-4	
1063 010-1	GZ	1063 027-5	LZ	1063 043-2	
1063 011-9	GZ	1063 028-3	LZ	1063 044-0	
1063 012-7	GZ	1063 029-1	LZ	1063 045-7	
1063 013-5	IN	1063 030-9	WS	1063 046-5	
1063 014-3	BL	1063 031-7	IN	1063 047-3	
1063 015-0	BL	1063 032-5	IN	1063 048-1	
1063 016-8	BL	1063 033-3	IN	1063 049-9	
1063 017-6	BL				

CLASS 1064   Co–Co

A recent class still being evaluated which can be found in the various yards around Wien. Examples may be transferred to other parts of the system for further tests. 1064 007–010 have been ordered for delivery in 1989.

Built: 1984–85.
Builder-Mech Parts: Simmering-Graz-Pauker.
Builder-Elec. Parts: Elin/Siemens.
One Hour Rating: 2340 kW.   **Weight in Full Working Order:** 112.2 tonnes
Maximum Tractive Effort: 370 kN.   **Length over Buffers:** 18.50 m.
Driving Wheel Dia.: 1145 mm.   **Max. Speed:** 80 km/h.

1064 001-9	WS	1064 005-0	WS	1064 008-4	
1064 002-7	VH	1064 006-8	WS	1064 009-2	
1064 003-5	WS	1064 007-6	WS	1064 010-0	
1064 004-3	WS				

CLASS 1067   C

Unusually for electric locomotives, these feature hydraulic transmission. Normally found on shunting and trip duties around Selzthal and sometimes at Hieflau/Eisenerz.

Built: 1963.
Builder-Mech Parts: Jenbach.
Builder-Elec. Parts: Elin.
One Hour Rating: 465 kW.   **Weight in Full Working Order:** 52.8 tonnes.
Maximum Tractive Effort: 245 kN.   **Length over Buffers:** 10.50 m.
Driving Wheel Dia.: 950 mm.   **Max. Speed:** 70 km/h.

1067 003-2	SL	1067 004-0	SL

CLASS 1080 E

This class is in the process of withdrawal. The main use is on pilot duties and transfer freights. SL locos can be found at Hieflau/Eisenerz, and Selzthal/Stainach Irdning, whilst those at AT see use over a wide area covering Summerau, St.Valentin, and Linz. There is an interesting Sunday only freight working from Linz (dep c. 07.30) to Summerau to effect a changeover of locos. 1080 011 was restored to original livery for the 1987 celebrations.

Built: 1924–25.
Builder-Mech Parts: Krauss.
Builder-Elec. Parts: Siemens, Wien.
One Hour Rating: 1020 kW.　　　　　**Weight in Full Working Order**: 77 tonnes.
Maximum Tractive Effort: 189 kN.　　**Length over Buffers**: 12.75 m.
Driving Wheel Dia.: 1350 mm.　　　　**Max. Speed**: 50 km/h.

1080 001-9 **G**	SL	1080 007-6 **G**	SL	1080 012-6 **G**	AT
1080 006-8 **G**	AT	1080 011-8 **G**	AT	1080 015-9	SL

CLASS 1180 E

As with class 1080, this class is also being withdrawn. Used on pilot duties at Bludenz, Bregenz, Wolfurt, Feldkirch and Landeck. Local freights are used as a means of changing over locos. Deliveries of cl. 1063 are leading to altered duties.

Built: 1926–27.
Builder-Mech Parts: Krauss.
Builder-Elec. Parts: Siemens-Wien.
One Hour Rating: 1300 kW.　　　　　**Weight in Full Working Order**: 80.5 tonnes.
Maximum Tractive Effort: 197 kN.　　**Length over Buffers**: 12.75 m.
Driving Wheel Dia.: 1350 mm.　　　　**Max. Speed**: 50 km/h.

1180 003-4 **G**	BL	1180 005-9 **G**	BL	1180 009-1 **G**	LK
1180 004-2 **G**	BL	1180 007-5 **G**	BL		

CLASS 1822 Bo–Bo

A new design whose external lines are based on the modern Swiss locos recently delivered by SLM to the Bodensee Toggenburg Bahn. The 1822s are intended for operation on the corridor trains from Lienz to Innsbruck via San Candido and will be dual voltage to allow them to work off Italian Railways 3000 V d.c. catenary. At one time some of the 1046s were reported to be earmarked for rebuilding for this route but a brand new design has been chosen instead. Delivery is due towards the middle of 1989. Two locos have been ordered at this stage.

Built:
Builder-Mech Parts:
Builder-Elec. Parts:
One Hour Rating: 4300 kW.　　　　　**Weight in Full Working Order**: 84 tonnes.
Maximum Tractive Effort:　　　　　**Length over Buffers**:
Driving Wheel Dia.:　　　　　　　　**Max. Speed**: 140 km/h.
Systems: 15 kV $16\frac{2}{3}$ Hz/3000 V d.c.

1822 001-2	1822 002-0

Class 1042 No. 1042 624-5 approaches the southern end of the Tauern Tunnel with a car-carrier shuttle train on 18/09/87. Note the auto-coupling on the locomotive to facilitate speedy run-rounds. Car drivers can remain in their cars.
Colin Boocock

DIESEL LOCOMOTIVES
CLASS 2043   BB

Although of relatively modest output, these locos are, along with class 2143, the most powerful diesels on the ÖBB. Utilisation is as follows:

GZ locos.: Graz–Szentgotthard and Hartberg.
KD locos.: St. Veit a. d. Glan–Hüttenberg. Zeltweg–Bleiburg–Klagenfurt.
LE locos.: Spittal–Lienz–San Candido–Brennero–Innsbruck.
LZ locos.: Linz–Aigen Schlagl/Bad Hall.
VH locos.: Villach–Kötschach Mauthen.
WE locos.: Wels to all non-electrified lines west of Wels.

2043 555–558 were rebuilt for working on the Vordernberg–Eisenerz line which is now closed. No announcement has been made as to the future use of these locos. They will probably be converted to standard. Lienz is likely to loose its allocation in late 1989 when the line from Lienz to San Candido is electrified. In all probability its locos will go to Krems to replace the 2045s.

Built: 1964–74.
Builder – Mech Parts: Jenbach.
Engine: Jenbach LM1500.
Power: 1100 kW (1475 hp) plus 224 kW (300 hp) for train heating.
Transmission: Hydraulic. Voith L830 rU2.
Maximum Tractive Effort: 196 kN.   **Weight in Full Working Order:** 68 tonnes.
Driving Wheel Dia.: 950 mm.   **Length over Buffers:** 14.76 (15.80*) m.
Train Heating: Electric.   **Max. Speed:** 110 (100*) km/h.

§ Magnetic track brakes for working Vordernberg–Eisenerz line (Erzbergbahn) now closed.

2043 001-3	*	KD	2043 027-8	GZ	2043 052-6	WE
2043 002-1	*	KD	2043 028-6	GZ	2043 053-4	LZ
2043 003-9	*	KD	2043 029-4	GZ	2043 054-2	LZ
2043 004-7	*	KD	2043 030-2	GZ	2043 059-1	LZ
2043 005-4		KD	2043 031-0	GZ	2043 060-9	LZ
2043 006-2		KD	2043 032-8	GZ	2043 061-7	LZ
2043 007-0 **N**		KD	2043 033-6	GZ	2043 062-5	LE
2043 008-8		KD	2043 034-4	GZ	2043 063-3	WE
2043 009-6		KD	2043 035-1	GZ	2043 064-1	LE
2043 010-4		KD	2043 036-9	GZ	2043 065-8	LE
2043 011-2		KD	2043 037-7	GZ	2043 066-6	LE
2043 012-0		KD	2043 038-5	GZ	2043 067-4 **N**	LE
2043 013-8		KR	2043 039-3	WE	2043 068-2	LE
2043 014-6		KR	2043 040-1	WE	2043 069-0	LE
2043 015-3		KR	2043 041-9	WE	2043 070-8	LE
2043 016-1		KR	2043 042-7	WE	2043 071-6	VH
2043 017-9		KR	2043 043-5	LZ	2043 073-2	VH
2043 018-7		WE	2043 044-3	LZ	2043 074-0	VH
2043 019-5		WE	2043 045-0	LZ	2043 075-7	VH
2043 020-3		WE	2043 046-8	LZ	2043 076-5	VH
2043 021-1		WE	2043 047-6	LE	2043 077-3	VH
2043 022-9		WE	2043 048-4	LE	2043 555-8 §	KD
2043 023-7		WE	2043 049-2	WE	2043 556-6 §	KD
2043 024-5		WE	2043 050-0	WE	2043 557-4 §	KD
2043 025-2		WE	2043 051-8	WE	2043 558-2 §	KD
2043 026-0		WE				

CLASS 2143   B–B

These locos are similar to class 2043 but were built by SGP. Uses:

GM locos.: Used between Gmünd and Krems and the various branches in between.
KR locos.: Work to St. Valentin and St. Pölten.
NS locos.: All lines radiating from there including corridor trains via Sopron.
WN locos.: Used on various non-electrified lines around Wien including Bruck a. d. Leitha to Wulkersprodersdorf.

Built: 1965–77.
Builder – Mech Parts: Simmering-Graz-Pauker.
Engine: SGP T12c.
Power: 1100 kW (1475 hp) plus 224 kW (300 hp) for train heating.
Transmission: Hydraulic. Voith L830 rU2.
Maximum Tractive Effort: 197 kN. **Weight in Full Working Order:** 65 (68m 67*) tonnes.
Driving Wheel Dia.: 950 mm. **Length over Buffers:** 15.76 m.
Train Heating: Electric. **Max. Speed:** 100 (110*) km/h.

m Fitted for multiple working.

2143 001-2 **N** *	NS	2143 028-5	NS	2143 053-3	m	GM
2143 003-8 *	NS	2143 029-3	NS	2143 054-1	m	GM
2143 004-6	NS	2143 030-1	NS	2143 055-8	m	GM
2143 005-3 **N**	NS	2143 031-9	NS	2143 056-6	m	WN
2143 006-1	NS	2143 032-7	NS	2143 057-4	m	WN
2143 007-9 **N**	NS	2143 033-5	NS	2143 058-2	m	WN
2143 008-7 **N**	NS	2143 034-3	m NS	2143 059-0	m	WN
2143 009-5	NS	2143 035-0	m KR	2143 060-8	m	WN
2143 010-3 **N**	NS	2143 036-8	m KR	2143 061-6	m	WN
2143 011-1	NS	2143 037-6	m KR	2143 062-4	m	WN
2143 012-9	NS	2143 038-4 **N**	m KR	2143 063-2	m	WN
2143 013-7	NS	2143 039-2	m KR	2143 064-0	m	WN
2143 014-5	NS	2143 040-0	m KR	2143 065-7	m	WN
2143 015-2	NS	2143 041-8	m KR	2143 066-5	m	WN
2143 016-0	NS	2143 042-6	m KR	2143 067-3	m	WN
2143 017-8	NS	2143 043-4	m GM	2143 068-1	m	WN
2143 018-6	NS	2143 044-2 **N**	m GM	2143 069-9	m	WN
2143 019-4	NS	2143 045-9	m GM	2143 070-7	m	WN
2143 020-2	NS	2143 046-7	m GM	2143 071-5	m	WN
2143 021-0	NS	2143 047-5	m GM	2143 072-3	m	WN
2143 022-8	NS	2143 048-3	m GM	2143 073-1	m	WN
2143 023-6	NS	2143 049-1	m GM	2143 074-9	m	WN
2143 024-4	NS	2143 050-9	m GM	2143 075-6	m	WN
2143 025-1	NS	2143 051-7	m GM	2143 076-4	m	WN
2143 026-9	NS	2143 052-5 **N**	m GM	2143 077-2	m	NS
2143 027-7	NS					

CLASS 2045   Bo–Bo

The oldest ÖBB main-line diesel loco. class, now being withdrawn. All are now based at Krems and are used as pilots and trip engines at Sigsmundsherberg, Schwarzenau, Gmünd, St.Pölten and Amstetten. 2045 020 was restored to green livery for the 1987 Celebrations.

Built: 1952–55.
Builder – Mech Parts: Simmering-Graz-Pauker.
Engine: SGP S12a.
Power: 760 kW (1020 hp).
Transmission: Electric. Brown-Boveri.
Maximum Tractive Effort: 152 kN. **Weight in Full Working Order:** 70.3 tonnes.
Driving Wheel Dia.: 960 mm. **Length over Buffers:** 14.80 m.
Train Heating: Steam. **Max. Speed:** 80 km/h.

2045 001-1	KR	2045 011-0	KR	2045 017-7	KR
2045 002-9	KR	2045 012-8	KR	2045 019-3	KR
2045 007-8	KR	2045 013-6	KR	2045 020-1 **G**	KR
2045 009-4	KR	2045 015-1	KR		

CLASS 2050   Bo–Bo

Until quite recently all the class were allocated in Wien for miscellaneous freight workings in the greater Wien area especially to Breclav, Mistelbach, Bruck a.d. Leitha. There are also odd passenger workings for which 2050 002 has train heating equipment. Those at Knittelfeld are fitted for multiple unit operation for heavy freight trains on the line to Pöls. 2050 002 was restored to green livery for the 1987 celebrations.

Built: 1958–62.
Builder – Mech Parts: Henschel.
Engine: GM 567C.
Power: 1050 kW (1408 hp).
Transmission: Electric.

Maximum Tractive Effort: 179 kN.	**Weight in Full Working Order:** 74.9 tonnes.
Driving Wheel Dia.: 1040 mm.	**Length over Buffers:** 17.76 m.
Max. Speed: 100 km/h.	**Train Heating:** Electric (2050 002-1 only).

2050 001-3	WN	2050 007-0	WN	2050 013-8	WN
2050 002-1 **G**	WN	2050 008-8	WN	2050 014-6	WN
2050 003-9	WN	2050 009-6	WN	2050 015-3	WN
2050 004-7	WN	2050 010-4	WN	2050 016-1	KD
2050 005-4	WN	2050 011-2	WN	2050 017-9	KD
2050 006-2	WN	2050 012-0	WN	2050 018-7	KD

CLASS 2060 B

These locos. perform light shunting duties all over the system.

Built: 1954–62. .
Builder – Mech Parts: Jenbach.
Engine: JW 200.
Power: 150 kW (200 hp).
Transmission: Hydraulic. Voith L33 yUB.
Maximum Tractive Effort: 100 kN. **Weight in Full Working Order:** 27 tonnes.
Driving Wheel Dia.: 950 mm. **Length over Buffers:** 6.68 m.
Max. Speed: 60 km/h.

2060 001-1	WL	2060 036-7	WE	2060 069-8	SP
2060 002-9	WL	2060 037-5	BO	2060 070-6	SP
2060 004-5	WN	2060 038-3	BO	2060 071-4	NS
2060 005-2	WN	2060 039-1	BO	2060 072-2	NS
2060 006-0	WN	2060 040-9	SL	2060 073-0	NS
2060 007-8	AT	2060 041-7	SL	2060 074-8	NS
2060 008-6	GZ	2060 042-5	SB	2060 075-5	NS
2060 009-4	IN	2060 043-3	SB	2060 076-3	NS
2060 010-2	IN	2060 044-1	SB	2060 077-1	VH
2060 011-0	IN	2060 045-8	SB	2060 078-9	AM
2060 012-8	IN	2060 046-6	SB	2060 079-7	AM
2060 013-6	IN	2060 047-4	VH	2060 080-5	AM
2060 014-4	IN	2060 048-2	VH	2060 081-3	WN
2060 015-1	LZ	2060 049-0	VH	2060 082-1	WN
2060 016-9	LZ	2060 050-8	VH	2060 083-9	WN
2060 017-7	LZ	2060 051-6	VH	2060 084-7	WN
2060 018-5	LZ	2060 052-4	VH	2060 085-4	WN
2060 019-3	LZ	2060 053-2	KD	2060 086-2	WN
2060 020-1	LZ	2060 054-0	KD	2060 087-0	WN
2060 021-9	LZ	2060 055-7	VH	2060 088-8	WN
2060 022-7	LZ	2060 056-5	KD	2060 089-6	WN
2060 023-5	LZ	2060 057-3	KD	2060 090-4	WN
2060 024-3	SL	2060 058-1	KD	2060 091-2	WN
2060 025-0	SL	2060 059-9	GZ	2060 092-0	WN
2060 026-8	SL	2060 060-7	GZ	2060 093-8	WN
2060 027-6	SL	2060 061-5	GZ	2060 094-6	WN
2060 029-2	AT	2060 062-3	GZ	2060 095-3	WN
2060 030-0	AT	2060 063-1	GZ	2060 096-1	BL
2060 031-8	AT	2060 065-6	SP	2060 097-9	BL
2060 032-6	AT	2060 066-4	SP	2060 098-7	BL
2060 033-4	WE	2060 067-2	SP	2060 099-5	BL
2060 034-2	WE	2060 068-0	SP	2060 100-1	BL
2060 035-9	WE				

Diesel-hydraulic shunter 2062 042-3 shunts the Wien Süd breakdown crane at Wiener Neustadt on 16/09/87.   *Colin Boocock*

CLASS 2062   B

These are medium powered shunters for use all over the system.

Built: 1958–66.
Builder – Mech Parts: Jenbach.
Engine: JW 400.
Power: 300 kW (402 hp).
Transmission: Hydraulic. Voith L26 St/A100 KV.
Maximum Tractive Effort: 120 kN.   **Weight in Full Working Order:** 32.3 tonnes.
Driving Wheel Dia.: 950 mm.   **Length over Buffers:** 7.92 m.
Max. Speed: 60 km/h.

2062 001-9	LZ	2062 023-3	GZ	2062 045-6	MZ
2062 002-7	LZ	2062 024-1	GZ	2062 046-4	WO
2062 003-5	LZ	2062 025-8	IN	2062 047-2	WO
2062 004-3	LZ	2062 026-6	IN	2062 048-0	MZ
2062 005-0	LZ	2062 027-4	IN	2062 049-8	MZ
2062 006-8	LZ	2062 028-2	IN	2062 050-6	MZ
2062 007-6	LZ	2062 029-0	LE	2062 051-4	MZ
2062 008-4	IN	2062 030-8	VH	2062 052-2	WO
2062 009-2	LZ	2062 031-6	SP	2062 053-0	WO
2062 010-0	VH	2062 032-4	SP	2062 054-8	WO
2062 011-8	VH	2062 033-2	SP	2062 055-5	WO
2062 012-6	VH	2062 034-0	SP	2062 056-3	WO
2062 013-4	VH	2062 035-7	SP	2062 057-1	WO
2062 014-2	VH	2062 036-5	WO	2062 058-9	WO
2062 015-9	VH	2062 037-3	WO	2062 059-7	WO
2062 016-7	KD	2062 038-1	WO	2062 060-5	WO
2062 017-5	KD	2062 039-9	WO	2062 061-3	WO
2062 018-3	KD	2062 040-7	NS	2062 062-1	WO
2062 019-1	KD	2062 041-5	NS	2062 063-9	WO
2062 020-9	KD	2062 042-3	NS	2062 064-7	WO
2062 021-7	GZ	2062 043-1	NS	2062 065-4	WO
2062 022-5	GZ	2062 044-9	MZ		

CLASS 2066   C

Usually employed as the Floridsdorf or Jedlersdorf Works shunter.

Built: 1954 (Rebuilt).
Builder – Mech Parts: ÖBB HW St.Pölten.
Engine: SGP 56P.
Power: 150 kW (201 hp).
Transmission: Electric.
Maximum Tractive Effort: 98 kN.   **Weight in Full Working Order:** 37 tonnes.
Driving Wheel Dia.: 950 mm.   **Length over Buffers:** 7.90 m.
Max. Speed: 40 km/h.

2066 001-5   WN

CLASS 2067   C

These are heavy duty diesel shunters which are found at Wels, Wien and Graz in use on the humps in pairs. They may be displaced from these duties by class 1063 deliveries.

Built: 1959–77.
Builder – Mech Parts: Simmering-Graz-Pauker.
Engine: SGP S12a.
Power: 450 kW (603 hp).
Transmission: Hydraulic. Voith L28.
Maximum Tractive Effort: 147 kN.   **Weight in Full Working Order:** 48.3 tonnes.
Driving Wheel Dia.: 1140 mm.   **Length over Buffers:** 10.34 m.
Max. Speed: 65 km/h.

m Fitted for multiple working.

2067 001-4	VH	2067 002-2		VH	2067 003-0		VH
2067 004-8	VH	2067 040-2		KD	2067 076-6		WE
2067 005-5	VH	2067 041-0		KD	2067 077-4		WE
2067 006-3	VH	2067 042-8	m	KD	2067 078-2		WE
2067 007-1	VH	2067 043-6	m	KD	2067 079-0		WE
2067 008-9	VH	2067 044-4	m	KD	2067 080-8		WE
2067 009-7	VH	2067 045-1	m	KD	2067 081-6		WE
2067 010-5	VH	2067 046-9	m	KD	2067 082-4		WO
2067 011-3	VH	2067 047-7	m	GZ	2067 083-2		WO
2067 012-1	GZ	2067 048-5	m	GZ	2067 084-0		WO
2067 013-9	GZ	2067 049-3	m	GZ	2067 085-7		WO
2067 014-7	GZ	2067 050-1		MZ	2067 086-5		WO
2067 015-4	GZ	2067 051-9		NS	2067 087-3		WO
2067 016-2	GZ	2067 052-7		NS	2067 088-1		WO
2067 017-0	SB	2067 053-5		NS	2067 089-9		WO
2067 018-8	SB	2067 054-3		NS	2067 090-7		WO
2067 019-6	SB	2067 055-0		LZ	2067 091-5		WO
2067 020-4	SB	2067 056-8		LZ	2067 092-3		WO
2067 021-2	SB	2067 057-6		WL	2067 093-1		WO
2067 022-0	SB	2067 058-4		BL	2067 094-9		WO
2067 023-8	SB	2067 059-2		BL	2067 095-6		WO
2067 024-6	LZ	2067 060-0		BL	2067 096-4		WO
2067 025-3	LZ	2067 061-8		BL	2067 097-2		WO
2067 026-1	LZ	2067 062-6		BL	2067 098-0		WO
2067 027-9	LZ	2067 063-4		BL	2067 099-8		WO
2067 028-7	LZ	2067 064-2		IN	2067 100-4		WO
2067 029-5	LZ	2067 065-9		IN	2067 101-2	m	WO
2067 030-3	LZ	2067 066-7		IN	2067 102-0	m	WO
2067 031-1	LZ	2067 067-5		IN	2067 103-8	m	WO
2067 032-9	LZ	2067 068-3		KD	2067 104-6	m	WO
2067 033-7	LZ	2067 069-1		WE	2067 105-3	m	WO
2067 034-5	LZ	2067 070-9		WE	2067 106-1	m	WO
2067 035-2	LZ	2067 071-7		WE	2067 107-9	m	WO
2067 036-0	WL	2067 072-5		WE	2067 108-7	m	WO
2067 037-8	AM	2067 073-3		WE	2067 109-5	m	WO
2067 038-6	AM	2067 074-1		WE	2067 110-3	m	WO
2067 039-4	AM	2067 075-8		WE	2067 111-1	m	WO

CLASS 2068 B–B

A new diesel shunter is under development and 5 prototypes are expected to appear soon.

Built: 1989.
Builder – Mech Parts: Jenbacher Werke.
Engine: JW 480 D.
Power: 820 kW (1100 hp) at 1500 rpm.
Transmission: Hydraulic. Voith L4r4zsU2.
Maximum Tractive Effort: 147 kN.　**Weight in Full Working Order:** 75.5 tonnes.
Driving Wheel Dia.: 950 mm.　**Length over Buffers:** 13.30 m.
Max. Speed: 100 km/h.
Multiple Working: With one other member of the same class.

2068 001-3	2068 003-9	2068 005-4
2068 002-1	2068 004-7	

CLASS 2080   B

This is a self-propelled snow-clearing machine.

Built: 1975.
Builder: Beilhack.
Engine: Deutz BF 12L413.
Power: 260 kW (350 hp).
Transmission: Hydraulic.
Snowplough Power: 2 x 310 kW.   **Weight in Full Working Order:** 42 tonnes.
Driving Wheel Dia.: 1000 mm.   **Length over Buffers:** 12.35 m.

Max. Speed: 80 km/h.

2080 001-7   IN |

CLASS 2180   B

Another self-propelled snow-clearing machine.

Built: 1982.
Builder – Mech Parts: Beilhack.
Engine:
Power: 370 kW (496 hp).
Transmission: Hydraulic.
Snowplough Power: 2 x 370 kW.   **Weight in Full Working Order:** 43 tonnes.
Driving Wheel Dia.: 1000 mm.   **Length over Buffers:** 12.35 m.
Max. Speed: 80 km/h.

2180 001-6   VH |

The largest of the ÖBB's diesel-hydraulic shunter classes is the 2067. 2067 054-3 is seen shunting at Wiener Neustadt on 19/09/87.   *Colin Boocock*

ELECTRIC MULTIPLE UNITS
CLASS 4010   6-CAR UNITS

These are Inter-City EMUs originally built for the "Transalpin" service. They now work over all principal routes, but the Transalpin service is now loco-hauled. The formations are normally constant but variations do occur at times of failures or for special reasons. It is not uncommon for tail vehicles to be attached as a means of strengthening over the easier routes. The WW sets have workings to München Hbf.

D4hET + B4hTI + B4hTI + BR4hTI (WR4hTI§) + AB4hTI + AD4hES (DMLV–TSO–TSK–TRSB (TRSS*, TRUB§)–TCK (with train telephone)–DTBFO.

Built: 1965–78.
Builder-Mech Parts: Simmering-Graz-Pauker.
Builder-Elec. Parts: Brown-Boveri/Siemens/Elin.
Traction Motors: 4 x 620 kW.
Seats: 0 + 60S 2L 2W + 66S 2L + 9S 34U (42U*, 36S 17U (loose chairs)§) + 24F 36S 2L + 42F 1L 1W.
Weight: 70.8 + 40 + 42 + 44 + 42 + 41 tonnes.
Length over Buffers: 16.82 + 26.4 + 26.4 + 26.4 + 26.4 + 26.7 m.
Max. Speed: 150 (160†) km/h.

```
4010 001-8 7010 101-9 7110 101-8 7310 001-8 7110 201-6 6010 001-3 T        WS
4010 002-6 7010 102-7 7110 102-6 7310 002-6 7110 202-4 6010 002-1 T        WS
4010 003-4 7010 103-5 7110 103-4 7310 003-4 7110 203-2 6010 003-9 T        WS
4010 004-2 7010 104-3 7110 104-2 7310 004-2 7110 204-0 6010 004-7 T        WS
4010 005-9 7010 105-0 7110 105-9 7310 005-9 7110 205-7 6010 005-4 T        WS
4010 006-7 7010 106-8 7110 106-7 7110 301-4 7110 206-5 6010 006-2 T *      WS
4010 007-5 7010 107-6 7110 107-5 7110 302-2 7110 207-3 6010 007-0 T *      WS
4010 008-3 7010 108-4 7110 108-3 7110 303-0 7110 208-1 6010 008-8 T *      WS
4010 009-1 7010 109-2 7110 109-1 7110 304-8 7110 209-9 6010 009-6 T *      WS
4010 010-9 7010 110-0 7110 110-9 7110 305-5 7110 210-7 6010 010-4 T *      GZ
4010 011-7 7010 111-8 7110 111-7 7110 306-3 7110 211-5 6010 011-2 T *      GZ
4010 012-5 7010 112-6 7110 112-5 7110 307-1 7110 212-3 6010 012-0 T *      GZ
4010 013-3 7010 113-4 7110 113-3 7110 308-9 7110 213-1 6010 013-8 T *      GZ
4010 014-1 7010 114-2 7110 114-1 7110 309-7 7110 214-9 6010 014-6 T *      GZ
4010 015-8 7010 115-9 7110 115-8 7110 310-5 7110 215-6 6010 015-3 T *      GZ
4010 016-6 7010 116-7 7110 116-6 7110 311-3 7110 216-4 6010 016-1 T *      GZ
4010 017-4 7010 117-5 7110 117-4 7110 312-1 7110 217-2 6010 017-9 T *      GZ
4010 018-2 7010 118-3 7110 118-2 7310 106-5 7110 218-0 6010 018-7 T §      WW
4010 019-0 7010 119-1 7110 119-0 7310 107-3 7110 219-8 6010 019-5 T §      WW
4010 020-8 7010 120-9 7110 120-8 7310 108-1 7110 220-6 6010 020-3 T §      WS
4010 021-6 7010 121-7 7110 121-6 7310 109-9 7110 221-4 6010 021-1 T §      WS
4010 022-4 7010 122-5 7110 122-4 7310 110-7 7110 222-2 6010 022-9 T §†     WW
4010 023-2 7010 123-3 7110 123-2 7310 111-5 7110 223-0 6010 023-7 T §      WW
4010 024-0 7010 124-1 7110 124-0 7310 112-3 7110 224-8 6010 024-5 T §      WW
4010 025-7 7010 125-8 7110 125-7 7310 113-1 7110 225-5 6010 025-2 T §      WW
4010 026-5 7010 126-6 7110 126-5 7310 114-9 7110 226-3 6010 026-0 T §      WW
4010 027-3 7010 127-4 7110 127-3 7310 115-6 7110 227-1 6010 027-8 T §      WW
4010 028-1 7010 128-2 7110 128-1 7310 116-4 7110 228-9 6010 028-6 T §†     WW
4010 029-9 7010 129-0 7110 129-9 7310 117-2 7110 229-7 6010 029-4 T §      WW
```

CLASS 4020   3-CAR UNITS

The new suburban EMU. Most are employed in the Wien area but some are now allocated to Linz, Innsbruck and Bludenz to bring some modern units onto the local services in those areas. Formations rarely vary.

B4hET + B4hTI + B4hES (DMSO–TSO–DTSO).

Built: 1978–87.
Builder-Mech Parts: Simmering-Graz-Pauker.
Builders-Elec. Parts: Brown Boveri/Elin/Siemens.
Traction Motors: 4 x 300 kW.